Make In Minutes

Cheesy Chicken & Rice Casserole

Prep: 5 min. Bake: 45 min.

1 can (10 3/4 oz.) Campbell's®
  Cream of Chicken (Regular *or* 98% Fat Free)
1 bag *uncooked* Success® White Rice (3/4 cup)
1 1/3 cups water
2 cups fresh *or* frozen vegetables
1/2 tsp. onion powder
4 skinless, boneless chicken breast halves
1/2 cup shredded Cheddar cheese

1. Stir the soup, rice, water, vegetables and onion powder in a 12" x 8" shallow baking dish.
2. Top with chicken. Season chicken as desired. Cover.
3. Bake at 375ºF, for 45 min. or until done. Top with cheese. Makes 4 servings.

Taste of Italy: In place of onion powder, use 1 tsp. Italian seasoning. Substitute 1/3 cup shredded Parmesan cheese for Cheddar.

Mexican Fiesta: In place of onion powder, use 1 tsp. chili powder. Substitute Mexican cheese blend for Cheddar.

Visit campbellskitchen.com & successrice.com for more delicious recipes.

HOME COOKING FROM A
YANKEE KITCHEN

A New England Harvest for all Seasons

HOME COOKING FROM A
YANKEE KITCHEN

A NEW ENGLAND HARVEST FOR ALL SEASONS

CONSULTANT EDITOR: LINDLEY BOEGEHOLD

SMITHMARK

This edition published in 1995 by
SMITHMARK Publishers Inc.
16 East 32nd Street
New York, NY 10016

SMITHMARK books are available for bulk purchase for sales promotion and for premium use.
For details write or call the Manager of Special Sales, SMITHMARK Publishers Inc., 16 East 32nd Street,
New York, NY, 10016; (212) 532-6600.

ISBN 0 8317 7456 8

Publisher: Joanna Lorenz
Editorial Manager: Helen Sudell
Designer: Nigel Partridge
Photographer: Amanda Haywood and Allan Montaine, Picture Perfect, USA (pp 6/7)
Recipes by: Carla Capalbo and Laura Washburn
Illustrations by: Estelle Corke

Printed in Singapore by Star Standard Industries Pte. Ltd.

Contents

"SOON AFTER RETURNING FROM OUR WALK, WE SAT DOWN AROUND A TABLE ABUNDANTLY SUPPLIED. THERE WAS A SUPERB PIECE OF CORNED BEEF, A STEWED GOOSE, AND A MAGNIFICENT LEG OF MUTTON, WITH VEGETABLES OF EVERY DESCRIPTION, AND AT THE END OF EACH TABLE, TWO LARGE JUGS OF CIDER, OF WHICH I NEVER TIRE OF DRINKING."

A DESCRIPTION OF A MEAL ENJOYED ON A FARM IN HARTFORD, CONNECTICUT AT THE END OF THE 18TH CENTURY.

FROM *THE PHYSIOLOGY OF TASTE* BY ANTHELME BRILLAT-SAVARIN

New England Clam Chowder

This classic Yankee soup will bring the seashore right into your kitchen. Serve it with crumbled saltines for the full experience.

SERVES 8

4 dozen cherrystone or littleneck clams, scrubbed

6 cups water

¼ cup finely diced salt pork or bacon

1½ cups minced onions

1 bay leaf

2½ cups diced peeled potatoes

salt and pepper

2 cups milk, warmed

1 cup light cream

chopped fresh parsley, for garnishing

Rinse the clams well in cold water. Drain. Place them in a deep kettle with the 6 cups of water and bring to a boil. Cover and steam the clams until the shells open, about 10 minutes. Remove from the heat.

When the clams have cooled slightly, remove them from their shells. Discard any clams that have not opened. Chop the clams coarsely. Strain the cooking liquid through a strainer lined with cheesecloth,

and reserve it.

In a large heavy saucepan, fry the salt pork or bacon until it renders its fat and begins to brown. Add the onions and cook over low heat until softened, 8-10 minutes.

Add the bay leaf, potatoes, and clam cooking liquid. Stir. Bring to a boil and cook 5-10 minutes.

Stir in the chopped clams. Continue to cook until the potatoes are tender, stirring occasionally. Season with salt and pepper.

Reduce the heat to low and stir in the warmed milk and cream. Simmer very gently 5 minutes more. Discard the bay leaf, and taste and adjust the seasoning before serving, sprinkled with parsley.

COOK'S TIP

IF CLAMS HAVE BEEN DUG, PURGING HELPS TO RID THEM OF SAND AND STOMACH CONTENTS. PUT THEM IN A BOWL OF COLD WATER, SPRINKLE WITH ½ CUP CORNMEAL AND SOME SALT. STIR LIGHTLY AND LET STAND IN A COOL PLACE FOR 3-4 HOURS.

CHILLED ASPARAGUS SOUP

—

FRESH ASPARAGUS IS ONE OF THE TRUE HARBINGERS OF SPRING. THIS SOUP IS SERVED CHILLED, BUT IF A BLUSTERY REMINDER OF WINTER ARRIVES IT IS ALSO DELICIOUS HOT.

10

SERVES 6

2 pounds fresh asparagus
4 tablespoons butter or olive oil
1½ cups sliced leeks or scallions
3 tablespoons flour
6 cups chicken stock or water
salt and pepper
½ cup light cream or plain yogurt
1 tablespoon minced fresh tarragon or chervil

Cut the top 2½ inches off the asparagus spears. Blanch these tips in boiling water until just tender, 5-6 minutes. Drain. Cut each tip into 2 or 3 pieces, and set aside.

Trim the ends of the stalks, removing any brown or woody parts. Chop the stalks into ½ inch pieces.

Heat the butter or oil in a heavy saucepan. Add the leeks or scallions and cook over low heat until softened, 5-8 minutes. Stir in the chopped asparagus stalks, cover, and cook 6-8 minutes more.

Add the flour and stir well to blend. Cook 3-4 minutes, uncovered, stirring occasionally.

Add the stock or water (see left). Bring to a boil, stirring frequently, then reduce the heat and simmer 30 minutes. Season with salt and pepper.

Purée the soup in a food processor or blender. If necessary, strain it to remove any coarse fibers. Stir in the asparagus tips, most of the cream or yogurt, and the herbs. Chill well. Stir thoroughly before serving, and check the seasoning. Garnish with swirled cream or yogurt.

COOK'S TIP

FOR A SMOOTHER TEXTURE, REMOVE THE "SCALES" OF THE ASPARAGUS SPEARS WITH A VEGETABLE PEELER.

MELON AND CRAB MEAT SALAD

—

THIS ELEGANT SALAD DEPENDS ON THE FRESHNESS OF ITS INGREDIENTS: MAKE SURE
THE MELON IS RIPE AND SWEET.

SERVES 6

1 pound fresh lump crab meat

½ cup mayonnaise

¼ cup sour cream or plain yogurt

2 tablespoons olive oil

2 tablespoons fresh lemon or lime juice

¼ cup minced scallions

2 tablespoons minced fresh cilantro

¼ teaspoon cayenne

salt and pepper

1½ canteloupe or small honeydew melons

3 medium-size heads of Belgian endive

fresh cilantro sprigs, for garnishing

Pick over the crab meat very carefully, removing any bits of shell or cartilage. Leave the pieces of crab meat as large as possible.

In a medium-size bowl, combine all the other ingredients except the melon and endive. Mix well (see above right). Fold the crab meat into this dressing.

Halve the melons and remove the seeds.

Cut into thin slices and remove the rind.

Arrange the salad on individual serving plates, making a decorative design with the melon slices and whole endive leaves. Place a mound of dressed crab meat on each plate. Garnish each salad with fresh cilantro sprigs.

VARIATIONS

FOR A LOBSTER SALAD, SUBSTITUTE 1 LARGE LOBSTER TAIL FOR THE CRAB MEAT. CHOP FINELY AND ADD IT TO THE REST OF THE INGREDIENTS, MIXING WELL.

FOR SHRIMP SALAD, SUBSTITUTE 1½ CUPS COARSELY CHOPPED COOKED SHRIMP.

OYSTER STEW

—

SERVES 6

2 cups milk

2 cups light cream

1 quart shucked oysters, drained, with their liquor reserved

⅛ teaspoon paprika

salt and pepper

2 tablespoons butter

1 tablespoon minced fresh parsley

 Combine the milk, cream, and oyster liquor in a heavy saucepan.

Heat the mixture over medium heat until small bubbles appear around the edge of the pan. Do not allow it to boil. Reduce the heat back down to low and add the oysters.

Cook, stirring occasionally, until the oysters plump up and their edges begin to curl. Add the paprika, and salt and pepper to taste.

Meanwhile, warm 6 soup plates or bowls. Cut the butter into 6 pieces and put one piece in the centre of each bowl.

Ladle in the oyster stew and sprinkle with parsley. Serve immediately, while still piping hot, with soda crackers if desired.

OYSTERS ROCKEFELLER

—

SERVES 6

1 pound fresh spinach leaves

½ cup chopped scallions

½ cup chopped celery

½ cup chopped fresh parsley

1 garlic clove

2 anchovy fillets

4 tablespoons butter or margarine

½ cup dry bread crumbs

1 teaspoon Worcestershire sauce

2 tablespoons anise-flavored liqueur (Pernod or Ricard)

½ teaspoon salt

hot pepper sauce

36 oysters in shell

fine strips of lemon rind, for garnishing

Wash the spinach well. Drain, and place in a heavy saucepan. Cover and cook over low heat until just wilted. Remove from the heat. When the spinach is cool enough to handle, squeeze it to remove excess water.

Put the spinach, scallions, celery, parsley, garlic, and anchovy fillets in a food processor and process until finely chopped.

Heat the butter or margarine in a skillet. Add the spinach mixture, bread crumbs, Worcestershire sauce, liqueur, salt, and hot pepper sauce to taste. Cook 1-2 minutes. Let cool, and refrigerate until ready to use.

Preheat the oven to 450°F. Line a baking sheet with crumpled foil.

Open the oysters and remove the top shells. Arrange them, side by side, on the foil (this will help keep them upright). Spoon all the spinach mixture over the oysters, smoothing the tops with the back of the spoon.

Bake until piping hot, about 20 minutes. Serve immediately, garnished with lemon rind.

COOK'S TIP

TO OPEN AN OYSTER PUSH THE POINT OF AN OYSTER KNIFE ABOUT ½ INCH INTO THE "HINGE". PUSH DOWN FIRMLY. THE LID SHOULD POP OPEN.

CAPE COD FRIED CLAMS

IN THE SUMMER ALL ALONG THE CAPE TINY ROAD SIDE STANDS SELL DELICIOUS, PIPING HOT FRIED CLAMS ACCOMPANIED BY A PAPER CUP FULL OF TARTARE SAUCE. THIS RECIPE ENABLES YOU TO RECREATE THE EXPERIENCE IN YOUR OWN KITCHEN.

SERVES 4

36 cherrystone clams, scrubbed

1 cup buttermilk

¼ teaspoon celery salt

¼ teaspoon cayenne

oil for deep-frying

1 cup dry bread crumbs

2 eggs, beaten with 2 tablespoons water

lemon wedges and tartare sauce or catsup, for serving

Rinse the clams well. Put them in a large kettle with 2 cups of water and bring to a boil. Cover and steam until the shells open.

Remove the clams from their shells (see below),

and cut away the black skins from the necks. Discard any clams that have not opened. Strain the cooking liquid and reserve.

Place the buttermilk in a large bowl and stir in the celery salt and cayenne. Add the clams and ½ cup of their cooking liquid. Mix well. Let stand 1 hour.

Heat oil in a deep-fryer or large saucepan to 375°F. (To test the temperature without a thermometer, drop in a cube of bread; it should be golden brown in 40 seconds.)

Drain the clams and roll them in the bread crumbs to coat all over. Dip them in the beaten egg and then in the bread crumbs again.

Fry the clams in the hot oil, a few at a time, stirring occasionally, until they are crisp and brown, about 2 minutes per batch. Remove with a slotted spoon and leave to drain on paper towels.

Serve the fried clams hot, accompanied by lemon wedges and tartare sauce or catsup.

SCALLOP AND MUSSEL KABOBS

—

GRILL THESE ELEGANT SEAFOOD KABOBS OUTDOORS IF THE WEATHER PERMITS, BUT MAKE SURE THE FIRE IS LOW AS SHELLFISH ARE DELICATE AND CAN OVERCOOK VERY QUICKLY.

18

SERVES 4

5 tablespoons butter, at room temperature
2 tablespoons minced fresh fennel fronds or parsley
1 tablespoon fresh lemon juice
salt and pepper
32 bay or small sea scallops
24 large mussels in shell
8 bacon slices
1 cup fresh bread crumbs
¼ cup olive oil
hot toast, for serving

Make the flavored butter by combining the butter with the minced herbs, lemon juice, and salt and pepper to taste. Mix well. Set aside.

In a small saucepan, cook the scallops in their own liquor until they begin to shrink. (If there is no scallop liquor – retained from the shells after shucking – use a little fish stock or white wine.) Drain and pat dry with paper towels.

Scrub the mussels well, and rinse under cold running water. Place in a large saucepan with about 1 inch of water in the bottom. Cover and steam the mussels over medium heat until they open. Remove them

from their shells, and pat dry on paper towels. Discard any mussels that have not opened.

Take 8 6-inch wooden or metal skewers. Thread on each one, alternately, 4 scallops, 3 mussels, and a slice of bacon, weaving the bacon between the scallops and mussels (see above).

Spread the bread crumbs on a plate. Lightly brush the seafood with olive oil and roll in the bread crumbs to coat all over.

Place the skewers on the broiler rack. Broil until crisp and lightly browned, 4-5 minutes on each side. Serve immediately with hot toast and the flavored butter.

EGGS BENEDICT

—

EXPERIMENT BY ADDING DIFFERENT COLORS AND TASTES TO THE RECIPE; ASPARAGUS OR
ARUGULA MAKE HEALTHY AND VISUALLY APPEALING SUBSTITUTES FOR THE HAM.

SERVES 4

1 teaspoon vinegar

4 eggs

2 English muffins or 4 rounds of bread

butter, for spreading

2 slices of cooked ham, ¼ inch thick, each cut in
*   half crosswise*

fresh chives, for garnishing

FOR THE SAUCE

3 egg yolks

2 tablespoons fresh lemon juice

¼ teaspoon salt

½ cup (1 stick) butter

2 tablespoons light cream

pepper

For the sauce, put the egg yolks, lemon juice, and salt in the container of a food processor or blender. Blend 15 seconds.

Melt the butter in a small saucepan until it bubbles (do not let it brown). With the motor running, pour the hot butter into the food processor or blender through the feed tube in a slow, steady stream. Turn off the machine as soon as all the butter has been added.

Scrape the sauce into the top of a double boiler, over just simmering water. Stir until thickened, 2-3 minutes. (If the sauce curdles, whisk in 1 tablespoon of boiling water.) Stir in the cream and season with pepper to taste. Keep warm over the hot water.

Bring a shallow pan of water to a boil. Stir in the vinegar. Break each egg into a cup, then slide it carefully into the water. Delicately turn the white around the yolk with a slotted spoon. Cook until the egg is set to your taste, 3-4 minutes. Remove to paper towels to drain. Very gently cut any ragged edges off the eggs with a small knife or scissors.

While the eggs are poaching, split and toast the muffins or toast the bread slices. Lightly butter while still warm.

Place a piece of ham, which you may brown in butter if you wish, on each muffin half or slice of toast. Trim the ham to fit neatly. Place an egg on each ham-topped muffin. Spoon the warm sauce over the eggs, garnish with chives, and serve.

CRAB CAKES WITH TARTARE SAUCE

THE RICHNESS OF THE CRAB CAKES IS PERFECTLY SET OFF BY THE TART AND CREAMY SAUCE. SERVE THIS DISH WITH A CRISP GREEN SALAD AND A GLASS OF WHITE WINE, IT NEEDS NOTHING ELSE.

SERVES 4

1½ pounds fresh lump crab meat

1 egg, beaten

2 tablespoons mayonnaise

1 tablespoon Worcestershire sauce

1 tablespoon sherry wine

2 tablespoons minced fresh parsley

1 tablespoon minced fresh chives or dill

salt and pepper

3 tablespoons olive oil

FOR THE SAUCE

1 egg yolk

1 tablespoon white wine vinegar

2 tablespoons Dijon-style mustard

1 cup vegetable or peanut oil

2 tablespoons fresh lemon juice

¼ cup minced scallions

2 tablespoons chopped drained capers

¼ cup minced sour dill pickles

¼ cup minced fresh parsley

Pick over the crab meat, carefully removing any shell or cartilage. If you can, try to keep the pieces of crab meat as large as possible.

In a mixing bowl, combine the beaten egg with the mayonnaise, Worcestershire sauce, sherry wine, and herbs. Season with salt and pepper. Fold in the crab meat.

Divide the mixture into 8 portions and gently form each one into an oval cake. Place on a baking sheet between layers of wax paper and refrigerate at least 1 hour.

Meanwhile, make the sauce. In a medium-size bowl, beat the egg yolk with a wire whisk until smooth. Add the vinegar, mustard, and salt and pepper to taste, and whisk about 10 seconds to blend. Then whisk in the olive oil in a slow, steady stream (about 30 seconds).

Add the lemon juice, scallions, capers, pickles, and parsley and mix together well. Check the seasoning. Cover and chill.

Preheat the broiler.

Brush the crab cakes with the olive oil. Place on an oiled baking sheet, in one layer.

Broil 6 inches from the heat until golden brown, about 5 minutes on each side. Serve the crab cakes hot with the tartare sauce.

BAKED SCROD

—

THE PUNGENCY OF CAPERS COMBINED WITH GARLIC AND TOMATOES GIVES THIS SIMPLE FISH RECIPE SPARKLE. IT WORKS EQUALLY WELL WITH THE OILIER BLUEFISH.

24

SERVES 6

2½ pounds scrod or bluefish fillets, skinned

3 tablespoons olive oil

1 teaspoon drained capers

2 garlic cloves

2 medium-size ripe tomatoes, peeled, seeded, and finely diced

2 tablespoons minced fresh basil, or 2 teaspoons dried basil

salt and pepper

1 cup dry white wine

Preheat the oven to 400°F.

Arrange the fillets in one layer in a shallow oiled baking dish. Brush the fish with olive oil.

Chop the capers with the garlic. Mix with the tomatoes and basil. Season with salt and pepper.

Spoon this mixture over the fish (see above).

Pour in the wine. Bake until the fish is cooked, 15-20 minutes. Test for doneness with the point of a knife; the fish should look opaque in the center. Serve hot.

SCALLOPS THERMIDOR

THIS SINFULLY-RICH PREPARATION ORIGINATED WITH LOBSTER AS THE MAIN INGREDIENT, BUT PLUMP, FRESH SEA SCALLOPS ARE A MARVELOUS SUBSTITUTE.

26

SERVES 6

2 pounds sea scallops

½ cup flour

½ cup (1 stick) butter or margarine

1 cup quartered small mushrooms

½ cup fresh bread crumbs

2 tablespoons minced fresh parsley

2 tablespoons minced fresh chives

½ cup sherry wine

¼ cup cognac

1 teaspoon Worcestershire sauce

½ teaspoon salt

¼ teaspoon black pepper

1½ cups whipping cream

2 egg yolks

chives, for garnishing

Preheat the oven to 400°F.

Roll the scallops in the flour, shaking off the excess. Heat half of the butter or margarine in a medium-size skillet. Add the scallops and sauté until they are barely golden all over, about 3 minutes. Remove from the skillet and set aside.

Melt 2 more tablespoons of butter or margarine in the pan. Add the mushrooms and bread crumbs and sauté 3-4 minutes, stirring. Add the parsley, chives, sherry wine, cognac, Worcestershire sauce, salt, and pepper. Cook 3-4 minutes more, stirring well.

Add the cream, and cook another 3-4 minutes, stirring occasionally (see above). Remove from the heat and mix in the egg yolks. Fold in the scallops.

Divide the mixture among 6 greased individual gratin or other baking dishes. Or, if you prefer, put it all in one large shallow baking dish. Dot with the remaining 2 tablespoons of butter or margarine.

Bake until bubbling and lightly browned, approximately 10 minutes. Serve immediately, in the greased dishes. Garnish with chopped chives, if desired.

SPAGHETTI WITH CLAMS

—

THIS TASTY DISH IS WITNESS TO THE BENEVOLENT INFLUENCE OF ITALIAN COOKING ON THE YANKEE KITCHEN. CHOP A TOMATO INTO THE CLAM LIQUID FOR A BIT OF COLOR.

28

SERVES 4

24 hard-shell clams, such as
*   littlenecks, scrubbed*
1 cup water
½ cup dry white wine
salt and pepper
1 pound spaghetti, preferably Italian
5 tablespoons olive oil
2 garlic cloves, minced
3 tablespoons minced fresh parsley

Rinse the clams well in cold water and drain. Place in a large kettle with the water and wine and bring to a boil. Cover and steam until the shells open, about 6-8 minutes.

Discard any clams that have not opened. Remove the clams from their shells. If large, chop them roughly.

Strain the cooking liquid through a strainer lined with cheesecloth. Place in a small saucepan and bring to the boil. Continue to boil rapidly until the liquid has reduced by about half. Set aside.

Bring a large pot of water to a boil. Add 2 teaspoons of salt. When the water is boiling rapidly, add the spaghetti and stir well as it softens. Cook until the spaghetti is almost done, and still firm to the bite (check package directions for timing).

Meanwhile, heat the olive oil in a large skillet. Add the garlic and cook 2-3 minutes, but do not let it brown. Add the reduced clam liquid and the parsley. Let cook over low heat until the spaghetti is ready.

Drain the spaghetti. Add it to the skillet, raise the heat to medium, and add the clams (see above). Cook 3-4 minutes, stirring constantly to cover the spaghetti with the sauce and to heat the clams.

Season with salt and pepper and serve. No cheese is needed with this sauce.

FLOUNDER WITH CRAB

—

SERVES 6

4 tablespoons butter or margarine

¼ cup flour

1 cup fish stock, or ¾ cup
*   fish stock mixed with*
*   ¼ cup dry white wine*

1 cup milk

1 bay leaf

salt and pepper

12 flounder fillets, about 2½ pounds

1½ cups fresh crab meat, flaked

½ cup freshly grated Parmesan cheese

Preheat the oven to 425°F

In a medium-size heavy saucepan, melt the butter or margarine over medium heat. Stir in the flour and cook 2-3 minutes.

Pour in the fish stock (or mixed fish stock and wine) and the milk. Whisk until smooth.

Add the bay leaf. Raise the heat to medium-high and bring to a boil. Cook 3-4 minutes more. Remove the sauce from the heat, and add salt to taste. Keep hot.

Butter a large baking dish. Twist each fillet to form a "cone" shape (see above right) and arrange

in the dish. Sprinkle the crab meat over the fish. Pour the hot sauce evenly over the top and sprinkle with the cheese.

Bake until the top is golden brown and the fish is cooked, 10-12 minutes. Test for doneness with the point of a knife: the fish should be just opaque in the center. Serve hot.

VARIATIONS

OTHER FLAT WHITE FISH, SUCH AS SOLE, CAN BE SUB- STITUTED FOR THE FLOUNDER. RAW PEELED AND DEVEINED SHRIMP, CHOPPED IF LARGE, CAN BE USED INSTEAD OF CRAB MEAT.

MAINE BROILED LOBSTER DINNER

NOWHERE IN THE WORLD DO LOBSTERS COME AS CANTANKEROUS, THICK-SHELLED AND TENDER-FLESHED AS THEY DO ON THE COLD COAST OF MAINE. SAVE THE SHELLS TO MAKE BISQUE THE NEXT DAY.

32

SERVES 4

4 live lobsters, 1½ pounds each

3 tablespoons minced mixed fresh herbs, such as parsley, chives, and tarragon

1 cup (2 sticks) butter, melted and kept warm

8 ears of tender fresh corn, shucked

salt and pepper

lemon halves, for serving

Preheat the broiler.

Kill each lobster quickly by inserting the tip of a large chef's knife between the eyes.

Turn the lobster over onto its back and cut it in half, from the head straight down to the tail (see

below left). Remove and discard the hard sac near the head, and the intestinal vein that runs through the middle of the underside of the tail. All the rest of the lobster meat is edible.

Combine the minced herbs with the melted butter.

Place the lobster halves, shell side up, in a foil-lined broiler pan or a large roasting pan. (You may have to do this in two batches.) Broil for approximately 8 minutes. Turn the lobster halves over, brush generously with the herb butter, and broil for a further 7-8 minutes.

While the lobsters are cooking, drop the corn into a large pot of rapidly boiling water and cook until just tender, 4-7 minutes. Drain.

Serve the lobsters and corn hot, with salt, freshly ground black pepper, lemon halves, and individual bowls of herb butter.

COOK'S TIP

PROVIDE CRACKERS FOR THE CLAWS, EXTRA PLATES FOR COBS AND SHELLS, FINGER BOWLS AND LOTS OF NAPKINS.

SHRIMP SOUFFLÉ

THE TRICK TO A TENDER, HIGH-RISING SOUFFLÉ IS TO BEAT THE EGG WHITES UNTIL THEY ARE STIFF BUT NOT DRY. THE HEAT OF THE OVEN FORCES THEM TO EXPAND UP INTO A DRAMATIC GOLDEN PUFF.

SERVES 4-6

1 tablespoon dry bread crumbs

2 tablespoons butter or margarine

⅔ cup coarsely chopped cooked shrimp

1 tablespoon minced fresh tarragon or parsley

¼ teaspoon pepper

3 tablespoons sherry or dry white wine

For the soufflé mixture

3 tablespoons butter or margarine

2½ tablespoons flour

1 cup milk, heated

¾ teaspoon salt

4 egg yolks

5 egg whites

Butter a 6- or 8-cup soufflé mold. Sprinkle with the bread crumbs, tilting the mold to coat the bottom and sides evenly. Preheat the oven to 400°F.

Melt the butter or margarine in a small saucepan. Add the chopped shrimp and cook 2-3 minutes over low heat. Stir in the herbs, pepper, and wine and cook 1-2 minutes more. Raise the heat and boil rapidly to evaporate the liquid. Remove from the heat and set aside.

For the soufflé mixture, melt the butter or margarine in a medium-size heavy saucepan. Add the flour, blending well with a wire whisk. Cook over low heat 2-3 minutes. Pour in the hot milk and whisk vigorously until smooth. Simmer 2 minutes, still whisking. Stir in the salt.

Remove from the heat and immediately beat in the egg yolks, one at a time. Stir in the shrimp mixture.

In a large bowl, beat the egg whites until they form stiff peaks. Stir about one-quarter of the egg whites into the shrimp mixture. Gently fold in the rest of the egg whites.

Turn the mixture into the prepared mold. Place in the oven and turn the heat down to 375°F. Bake until the soufflé is puffed up and lightly browned on top, 30-40 minutes. Serve immediately.

VARIATIONS

FOR LOBSTER SOUFFLÉ, SUBSTITUTE 1 LARGE LOBSTER TAIL FOR THE COOKED SHRIMP. CHOP IT FINELY AND ADD TO THE SAUCEPAN WITH THE HERBS AND WINE IN PLACE OF THE SHRIMP. FOR CRAB SOUFFLÉ, USE 1 CUP FRESH LUMP CRAB MEAT, PICKED OVER CAREFULLY TO REMOVE ANY BITS OF SHELL, IN PLACE OF THE SHRIMP.

CHICKEN BRUNSWICK STEW

—

THIS HEARTY, WHOLESOME STEW IS FILLING, ECONOMICAL AND ALWAYS TASTES BETTER A DAY OR TWO AFTER IT HAS BEEN MADE. SERVE WITH A BAKED POTATO FOR A WARMING WINTER MEAL.

SERVES 6

4-pound broiler chicken, cut into serving pieces

salt and pepper

paprika

2 tablespoons olive oil

2 tablespoons butter

2 cups chopped onions

1 cup chopped green or yellow bell pepper

2 cups chopped peeled fresh or canned plum
  tomatoes

1 cup white wine

2 cups chicken stock or water

¼ cup chopped fresh parsley

½ teaspoon hot pepper sauce

1 tablespoon Worcestershire sauce

2 cups corn kernels (fresh, frozen, or canned)

1 cup lima beans (fresh or frozen)

3 tablespoons flour

biscuits, rice, or potatoes, for serving (optional)

Rinse the chicken pieces under cool water and pat dry with paper towels. Sprinkle each piece lightly with salt and paprika.

In a large heavy saucepan or Dutch oven, heat the olive oil with the butter over medium-high heat. Heat until the mixture is sizzling and just starting to change color.

Add the chicken pieces and fry until golden brown on all sides. Remove the chicken pieces with tongs and set aside.

Reduce the heat to low and add the onions and bell pepper. Cook until softened, 8-10 minutes.

Raise the heat. Add the tomatoes and their juice, the wine, stock or water, parsley, and hot pepper and Worcestershire sauces. Stir and bring to a boil.

Return the chicken to the pan, pushing it down in the sauce. Cover, reduce the heat, and simmer 30 minutes, stirring occasionally.

Add the corn and lima beans and mix well. Partly cover and cook 30 minutes more.

Tilt the pan, and skim off as much of the surface fat as possible. In a small bowl, mix the flour with a little water to make a paste.

Gradually stir in about ¾ cup of the hot sauce from the pan. Stir the flour mixture into the stew, and mix well to distribute it evenly. Cook 5-8 minutes more, stirring occasionally.

Check the seasoning. Serve the stew in shallow soup plates or large bowls, with biscuits, rice, or potatoes, if desired.

SCRAPPLE

THRIFTY YANKEES DEVELOPED THIS DISH TO MAKE USE OF EVERY LAST TIDBIT ON THE PIG.
IT IS A QUINTESSENTIAL NEW ENGLAND RECIPE.

SERVES 10

3 pounds pork neck bones or pigs' knuckles

3 quarts water

2 teaspoons salt

1 bay leaf

2 fresh sage leaves

1 teaspoon pepper

2¾ cups yellow cornmeal

*maple syrup, fried eggs, and broiled tomatoes, for
    serving (optional)*

Put the pork bones or knuckles, water, salt,
and herbs in a large pot. Bring to a boil and
simmer 2 hours.

Remove the meat from the bones and chop it
finely or grind it. Set aside. Strain the broth and
skim off any fat from the surface. Discard the bones.

Put 2 quarts of the
broth in a large
heavy saucepan.
Add the chopped or
ground meat and the
pepper. Bring to a boil.
There should be about
1 quart of broth left. Stir the cornmeal into this. Add to the boiling
mixture in the pan and cook until
thickened, about 10 minutes, stirring
constantly.

Reduce the heat to very low, cover the pan,
and continue cooking about 25 minutes, stirring
often. Check the seasoning.

Turn the mixture into 2 loaf pans, smoothing the
surface (as above). Cool, then refrigerate overnight.

To serve, cut the loaves into ½ inch slices.
Sprinkle with flour and brown on both sides in butter or other fat over medium heat. Serve with
warmed maple syrup, fried eggs, and broiled tomato halves, if desired.

YANKEE POT ROAST

—

THE INSERTION OF GARLIC INTO THE CHUCK ROAST GIVES THIS HOMELY, NEW ENGLAND DISH
A MEDITERRANEAN AIR.

SERVES 8

*4-pound chuck roast, or bottom
   round roast or brisket*
3 garlic cloves, cut in half or in thirds
½ pound piece of salt pork or slab bacon
2 cups chopped onions
1 cup chopped celery
1½ cups chopped carrots
1 cup diced turnips
2 cups beef or chicken stock
2 cups dry red or white wine
1 bay leaf
*1 teaspoon fresh thyme leaves, or ½ teaspoon dried
   thyme*
*8 small whole potatoes, or 2 large potatoes,
   quartered*
½ teaspoon salt
½ teaspoon pepper
*4 tablespoons butter or margarine, at room
   temperature*
¼ cup flour
watercress, for garnishing

Preheat the oven to 325°F.
With the tip of a sharp knife, make deep incisions in the chuck roast, on all sides, and insert the garlic pieces.

In a large flameproof casserole or Dutch oven, cook the salt pork or bacon over low heat until it renders its fat and begins to brown.

Remove the salt pork with a slotted spoon and discard. Raise the heat to medium-high and add the chuck roast. Brown it on all sides, stirring occasionally. Remove and set aside.

Add the onions, celery, and carrots to the casserole and cook over low heat until softened, 8-10 minutes. Stir in the turnips. Add the stock, wine, and herbs and mix well. Return the roast. Cover and place in the oven. Cook 2 hours.

Add the potatoes, pushing them down under the other vegetables. Season with salt and pepper. Cover again and cook until the potatoes are tender, about 45 minutes.

In a small bowl, combine the butter or margarine with the flour and mash together to make a paste.

Transfer the meat to a warmed serving platter. Remove the potatoes and other vegetables from the casserole with a slotted spoon and arrange around the roast. Keep hot.

Discard the bay leaf. Tilt the casserole and skim

off the excess fat from the surface of the cooking liquid. Bring to a boil on top of the stove. Add half of the butter and flour paste and whisk to blend. Cook until the gravy is thickened, 3-4 minutes. Add more of the paste if the gravy is not sufficiently thick. Strain into a gravy boat.

Serve with the sliced meat and vegetables, garnished with watercress.

RED FLANNEL HASH WITH CORNED BEEF

—

THERE IS NO MORE COMFORTING SUNDAY NIGHT SUPPER THAN THIS SIMPLE AND COLORFUL HASH. ALWAYS SERVE THIS HASH WITH PLENTY OF CATSUP. A FRIED EGG ON THE SIDE IS ALSO TRADITIONAL.

SERVES 4

6 bacon slices
¾ cup minced onion
2½ cups peeled, boiled, and diced potatoes
1½ cups chopped corned beef
1½ cups diced cooked beets (not in vinegar)
¼ cup light cream or half and half
¼ cup minced fresh parsley
salt and pepper

Cook the bacon in a large, heavy nonstick skillet until golden and beginning to crisp. Remove with a slotted spatula and leave to drain on paper towels. Pour off all but the last 2 tablespoons of the bacon fat in the pan, reserving the rest for later.

Cut the bacon into ½ inch pieces and place in a mixing bowl. Cook the onion in the bacon fat over low heat until softened, 8-10 minutes. Remove it from the pan and add to the bacon. Mix in the potatoes, corned beef, beets, cream, and the minced parsley. Season with salt and pepper and mix well.

Heat 4 tablespoons of the reserved bacon fat, or other fat, in the skillet. Add the hash mixture, spreading it evenly with a spatula. Cook over low heat until the base is brown, about 15 minutes. Flip the hash out onto a plate.

Gently slide the hash back into the skillet and continue to cook on the other side until lightly browned (see above).

Serve immediately.

BOSTON BAKED BEANS

—

SUGAR AND MUSTARD GIVE THIS HEARTY SIDE DISH AN IRRESISTIBLE SWEET-HOT FLAVOR.

44

SERVES 8

3 cups dried navy or Great Northern beans

1 bay leaf

4 cloves

2 medium-size onions, peeled

½ cup molasses

¾ cup dark brown sugar, firmly packed

1 tablespoon Dijon-style mustard

1 teaspoon salt

1 teaspoon pepper

1 cup boiling water

½ pound piece of salt pork

Rinse the beans under cold running water. Drain and place in a large bowl. Cover with cold water and let soak overnight.

Drain and rinse the beans. Put them in a large kettle with the bay leaf and cover with fresh cold water. Bring to a boil and then reduce heat and simmer until tender, 1½-2 hours. Drain.

Preheat the oven to 275°F

Put the beans in a large casserole. Stick 2 cloves in each of the onions and add them to the pot.

In a mixing bowl, combine the molasses, sugar, mustard, salt, and pepper. Add the boiling water and stir to blend.

Pour this mixture over the beans. Add more water if necessary so the beans are almost covered with liquid.

Blanch the piece of salt pork in boiling water for 3 minutes. Drain. Score the rind in deep ½ inch cuts (see below). Add the salt pork to the casserole and push below the surface of the beans, skin-side up.

Cover the casserole and bake in the center of the oven for 4½-5 hours. Uncover for the last half hour, so the pork rind becomes brown and crisp. Slice or shred the pork and serve hot.

HARVARD BEETS

—

SO CALLED BECAUSE OF THEIR COLOR —
HARVARD UNIVERSITY'S BEING CRIMSON.
SUBSTITUTE CANNED BEETS IF TIME IS SHORT.

SERVES 6

5 medium-size cooked beets (about 1½ pounds)

⅓ cup sugar

1 tablespoon cornstarch

½ teaspoon salt

¼ cup cider or white wine vinegar

½ cup beet cooking liquid or water

2 tablespoons butter or margarine

 Peel the beets and cut into medium-thick slices. Set aside.

In the top of a double boiler, combine all the other ingredients except the butter or margarine. Stir until smooth. Cook over hot water, stirring constantly, until the mixture is smooth and clear.

Add the beets and butter or margarine. Continue to cook over the hot water, stirring, until the beets are heated through, about 10 minutes. Serve hot.

COOK'S TIP

IF COOKING THE BEETS YOURSELF, CHOOSE THEM CARE-
FULLY. AVOID DAMAGED FLESH OR DRY PATCHES.

SWEET POTATO BISCUITS

—

LEFTOVER SWEET POTATOES WERE NEVER PUT TO BETTER USE. THESE LIGHT AND TENDER BISCUITS GO WELL WITH BAKED HAM OR ROAST CHICKEN.

46

MAKES ABOUT 24

1¼ cups flour

4 teaspoons baking powder

1 teaspoon salt

1 tablespoon brown sugar

¾ cup mashed cooked sweet potatoes

⅔ cup milk

4 tablespoons butter or margarine, melted

Preheat the oven to 450°F.

Sift the flour, baking powder, and salt into a bowl. Add the sugar and stir to mix.

In a separate bowl, combine the sweet potatoes with the milk and melted butter or margarine. Mix well until evenly blended.

Stir the dry ingredients into the sweet potato mixture to make a dough. Turn the mixture onto a lightly-floured surface and knead lightly just to mix, 1-2 minutes.

Roll out the dough to ½ inch thickness. Cut out rounds with a 1½-inch cookie cutter (see above).

Arrange the rounds on a greased cookie sheet, and bake until puffed and lightly golden, approximately 15 minutes.

Serve the biscuits warm.

FRIED TOMATOES

—

THIS RECIPE IS THE ONLY INCENTIVE TO PICKING TOMATOES WHILE THEY ARE STILL GREEN. WHEN SERVED HOT WITH BACON AND EGGS THEY BECOME THE GREATEST BREAKFAST IN THE WORLD — OR AT LEAST IN THE ORIGINAL **13** STATES.

48

SERVES 4

2-3 large green or very firm red tomatoes (about ½ pound)

⅓ cup flour

4 tablespoons butter or bacon fat

salt and pepper

sugar, if needed

4 slices of hot buttered toast

¾ cup half and half

 Slice the tomatoes into ½ inch rounds. Coat lightly with flour.

Heat the butter or bacon fat in a skillet. When it is hot, add the tomato slices and cook until browned. Turn them once, and season generously with salt and pepper.

If the tomatoes are green, sprinkle each slice with a little sugar. Cook until the other side is brown, 3-4 minutes more.

Divide the tomatoes among the slices of toast and keep hot.

VARIATION

FOR FRIED TOMATOES WITH HAM, TOP THE TOAST WITH HAM SLICES BEFORE COVERING WITH THE TOMATOES.

COLESLAW

—

HOMEMADE COLESLAW IS A THING OF BEAUTY; SWEET, SOUR, CRISP AND TENDER ALL AT ONCE. IT IS A CLASSIC SIDE DISH AT COOKOUTS.

SERVES 8

1 cup mayonnaise

½ cup white wine vinegar

1 tablespoon Dijon-style mustard

2 teaspoons sugar

1 tablespoon caraway seeds

salt and pepper

8 cups finely sliced green cabbage, or a mixture of green and red cabbage

1 cup grated carrots

1 cup finely sliced yellow or red onions

Combine the mayonnaise, vinegar, mustard, sugar, and caraway seeds. Season with salt and pepper.

Put the cabbage, carrots, and onions in a large bowl.

Add the dressing to the vegetables and mix well. Taste for seasoning. Cover and refrigerate for approximately 1-2 hours. The cabbage will become tastier and more tender the longer it marinates.

BOSTON BROWN BREAD

—

THIS UNUSUAL BREAD IS BAKED ENCLOSED IN A CAN WHICH KEEPS IT ESPECIALLY MOIST AND
DENSELY TEXTURED. IT IS AN ESSENTIAL PART OF THE CLASSIC BEANTOWN DINNER.

MAKES 2 SMALL LOAVES

1 tablespoon butter or margarine, at room
  temperature
1 cup yellow cornmeal
1 cup graham or whole-wheat flour
1 cup rye flour
2 teaspoons baking soda
1 teaspoon salt
2 cups buttermilk, at room temperature
¾ cup molasses
1 cup chopped raisins
butter or cream cheese, for serving

Grease two 1-pound food cans, or, alternatively, two 1-quart pudding molds, with the soft butter or margarine.

Sift all the dry ingredients together into a large bowl. Tip in any bran from the whole-wheat flour. Stir well to blend.

In a separate bowl, combine the buttermilk, molasses, and raisins. Add to the dry ingredients and mix well.

Pour the batter into the prepared molds, filling them about two-thirds full. Cover the tops with buttered foil, and tie or tape it down so that the rising

bread cannot push the foil lid off (see below).

Set the molds on a rack in a large kettle with a tight-fitting lid. Pour in enough warm water to come halfway up the sides of the molds. Cover the pan, bring to a boil, and steam for 2½ hours. Check occasionally that all the water has not boiled away, and add more if necessary.

Unmold the bread on a warmed serving dish. Slice and serve the bread with butter or cream cheese for spreading.

SHAKER SUMMER PUDDING

—

THE SHAKER COMMUNITY IS KNOWN FOR ITS TRADITION OF SIMPLE AND
ELEGANT HANDICRAFTS. THIS DELECTABLE BERRY DESSERT REFLECTS THE
SAME CHARACTER.

SERVES 6-8

*1 loaf of white farmhouse-type
bread, 1-2 days old, sliced*
1½ pounds fresh red currants
¼ cup plus 2 tablespoons sugar
¼ cup water
*1½ pounds berries; raspberries, blueberries, and
blackberries*
juice of ½ lemon
whipped cream, for serving (optional)

Trim the crusts from the bread slices. Cut a round of bread to fit in the bottom of a 6-cup domed pudding mold or mixing bowl. Line the sides of the mold with bread slices, cutting them to fit and overlapping them slightly. Reserve enough bread slices to cover the top of the mold.

Combine the red currants with ¼ cup sugar and water in a non-reactive saucepan. Heat gently, crushing the berries lightly to help the juices flow. As the sugar dissolves, remove from the heat.

Tip the currant mixture into a food processor and process until quite smooth. Press through a fine-mesh nylon strainer set in a bowl. Discard the fruit pulp left in the strainer.

Put the berries in a bowl with the remaining sugar and the lemon juice. Stir well.

One at a time, remove the cut bread pieces from the mold and dip in the red-currant purée. Replace to line the mold evenly.

Spoon the berries into the lined mold (see below), pressing down evenly. Top with the reserved bread slices, which have been dipped in the currant purée. Cover the mold with plastic wrap. Set a small plate, just big enough to fit inside the rim of the mold, on top of the pudding. Weigh it down with cans of food. Refrigerate 8-24 hours.

To unmold, remove the weights, plate, and plastic wrap. Run a knife between the mold and the pudding to loosen it. Turn out onto a serving plate. Serve in wedges, with whipped cream if desired.

PEACH AND BLUEBERRY PIE

—

THIS PIE MUST BE MADE WHEN PEACHES AND BLUEBERRIES ARE IN SEASON. ITS
FLAVOR IS IMPECCABLE, AND ZEALOTS HAVE BEEN KNOWN TO EAT LEFTOVERS FOR BREAKFAST.

54

SERVES 8

2 cups flour
½ teaspoon salt
2 teaspoons sugar
10 tablespoons (1¼ sticks) cold butter or margarine
1 egg yolk
¼ cup or more ice water
2 tablespoons milk, for glazing

FOR THE FILLING

3 cups peeled, pitted, and sliced fresh peaches
2 cups fresh blueberries

¾ cup sugar
2 tablespoons fresh lemon juice
⅓ cup flour
⅛ teaspoon grated nutmeg
2 tablespoons butter or margarine, cut in pea-size pieces

For the pastry, sift the flour, salt and sugar into a bowl. Using a pastry blender or 2 knives, cut the butter or margarine into the dry ingredients as quickly as possible until the mixture resembles coarse meal.

Mix the egg yolk with the ice water and sprinkle over the flour mixture. Combine with a fork until the dough holds together. If the dough is too crumbly, add a little more water, 1 tablespoon at a time. Gather the dough into a ball and flatten into a disk. Wrap in wax paper and refrigerate at least 20 minutes.

Roll out two-thirds of the dough between 2 sheets of wax paper to a thickness of about ⅛ inch. Use to line a 9-inch pie pan. Trim all around, leaving a ½ inch overhang. Fold the overhang under to form the edge. Using a fork, press the edge to the rim of the pie pan.

Gather the trimmings and remaining dough into a ball, and roll out to a thickness of about ¼ inch. Using a pastry wheel or sharp knife, cut strips ½ inch wide. Refrigerate both the pie shell and the strips of dough for 20 minutes.

Preheat the oven to 400°F.

Line the pie shell with wax paper and fill with dried beans. Bake until the pie shell is just set, 7-10 minutes. Remove from the oven and carefully lift out the paper with the beans. Prick the bottom of the pie shell all over with a fork, then return to the oven and bake 5 minutes more. Let the pie shell cool slightly before filling. Leave the oven on.

In a mixing bowl, combine the peach slices with the blueberries, sugar, lemon juice, flour, and nutmeg. Spoon the fruit mixture evenly into the pie shell. Dot with the pieces of butter or margarine.

Weave a lattice top with the pastry strips, pressing the ends to the edge. Brush the strips with milk.

Bake the pie 15 minutes. Reduce the heat to 350°F, and continue baking until the filling is tender and bubbling and the pastry lattice is golden, about 30 minutes more. If the pastry gets too brown, cover loosely with a piece of foil. Serve the pie warm or at room temperature.

BOSTON CREAM PIE

—

THIS HOMEMADE VERSION TASTES MUCH BETTER THAN THE UBIQUITOUS BAKERY DESSERT.
IT IS MORE LIKE A FROSTED CAKE THAN A PIE, BUT WHAT'S IN A NAME?

SERVES 8

2 cups cake flour

1 tablespoon baking powder

½ teaspoon salt

½ cup (1 stick) butter, at room temperature

1 cup granulated sugar

2 eggs

1 teaspoon vanilla extract

¾ cup milk

FOR THE FILLING

1 cup milk

3 egg yolks

½ cup granulated sugar

¼ cup flour

1 tablespoon butter

1 tablespoon brandy or 1 teaspoon vanilla extract

FOR THE CHOCOLATE GLAZE

1 ounce square unsweetened chocolate

2 tablespoons butter or margarine

½ cup confectioners' sugar, plus extra for
    dusting

½ teaspoon vanilla extract

about 1 tablespoon hot water

Preheat the oven to 375°F.

Grease 2 8 x 2-inch round cake pans, and line the bottoms with rounds of greased wax paper.

Sift the flour with the baking powder and salt.

Beat the butter and granulated sugar together until light and fluffy. Add the eggs one at a time, beating well after each addition. Stir in the vanilla. Add the milk and dry ingredients alternately, mixing only enough to blend thoroughly. Do not over-beat the batter.

Divide the cake batter between the prepared pans and spread it out evenly. Bake until a cake tester inserted in the center comes out clean, about 25 minutes.

Meanwhile, make the filling. Heat the milk in a small saucepan to boiling point. Quickly remove from the heat.

In a heatproof mixing bowl, beat the egg yolks smooth. Gradually add the granulated sugar and continue beating until pale yellow. Beat in the flour.

Pour the hot milk into the egg yolk mixture in a steady stream, beating constantly. When all the milk has been added, place the bowl over, not

in, a pan of boiling water, or pour the mixture into the top of a double boiler. Heat, stirring constantly, until thickened. Cook 2 minutes more, then remove from the heat. Stir in the butter and brandy or vanilla. Let cool.

When the cake layers have cooled, use a large sharp knife to slice off the domed tops to make a flat surface. Place one layer on a serving plate and spread on the filling in a thick layer. Set the other layer on top, cut side down. Smooth the edge of the filling layer so it is flush with the sides of the cake layers.

For the glaze, melt the chocolate with the butter or margarine in the top of a double boiler. When smooth, remove from the heat and beat in the sugar to make a thick paste. Add the vanilla. Beat in a little of the hot water. If the glaze does not have a spreadable consistency, add more water, 1 teaspoon at a time.

Spread the glaze evenly over the top of the cake, using a metal spatula. Dust the top with confectioners' sugar. Because of the custard filling, refrigerate any leftover cake.

APPLE BROWN BETTY

—

WHEN YOU DON'T HAVE TIME TO MAKE A PIE CRUST BUT WANT A COMFORTING, HEALTHY DESSERT THIS DISH FITS THE BILL. MACINTOSH OR CORTLAND APPLES ARE ESPECIALLY GOOD.

SERVES 6

1 cup fresh bread crumbs
¾ cup light brown sugar, firmly packed
½ teaspoon ground cinnamon
¼ teaspoon ground cloves
¼ teaspoon grated nutmeg
4 tablespoons butter
2 pounds tart-sweet apples
juice of 1 lemon
⅓ cup finely chopped walnuts

Preheat the broiler.

Spread the bread crumbs on a cookie sheet and toast under the broiler until golden, stirring so they color evenly. Set aside.

Preheat the oven to 375°F. Butter a 2-quart baking dish.

Mix the sugar with the spices. Cut the butter into pea-size pieces; set aside.

Peel, core, and slice the apples (about ¼ inch thick). Toss the apples immediately with the lemon juice to prevent the apple slices from turning brown (see right).

Sprinkle about 2½ tablespoons of bread crumbs over the bottom of the prepared dish. Cover with one-third of the apples and sprinkle with one-third of the sugar-spice mixture. Add another layer of bread crumbs and dot with one-third of the butter. Repeat the layers two more times, ending with a layer of bread crumbs. Sprinkle with the nuts, and dot with the remaining butter.

Bake until the apples are tender and the top is golden brown, 35-40 minutes. Serve warm. Good with cream or ice cream.

BRETHREN'S CIDER PIE

—

MAKE THIS DELICATELY-FLAVORED PIE IN THE FALL WHEN FRESH CIDER IS BEING SOLD
AT EVERY ROADSIDE STAND.

SERVES 6

1½ cups flour

¼ teaspoon salt

2 teaspoons sugar

½ cup (1 stick) cold butter or margarine

¼ cup or more ice water

FOR THE FILLING

2½ cups apple cider

1 tablespoon butter

1 cup maple syrup

¼ cup water

¼ teaspoon salt

2 eggs, at room temperature, separated

1 teaspoon grated nutmeg

For the pastry, sift the flour, salt, and sugar into a bowl. Using a pastry blender or 2 knives, cut the butter or margarine into the dry ingredients as quickly as possible until the mixture resembles coarse meal.

Sprinkle the ice water over the flour mixture. Combine with a fork until the dough holds together. If the dough is too crumbly, add a little more water, 1 tablespoon at a time. Gather the dough into a ball and flatten into a disk. Wrap in wax paper and refrigerate at least 20 minutes.

Meanwhile, place the cider in a medium-size heavy saucepan. Boil until only ¾ cup remains. Set aside and allow to cool.

Roll out the dough between 2 sheets of wax paper to a thickness of about ⅛ inch. Use to line a 9-inch pie pan.

Trim all around, leaving a ½ inch overhang. Fold the overhang under to form the edge. Using a fork, press the edge to the rim of the pan and press up from under with your fingers at intervals for a ruffle effect. Refrigerate 20 minutes.

Preheat the oven to 350°F.

For the filling, add the butter, maple syrup, water, and salt to the cider and simmer gently 5-6 minutes. Remove from the heat and let the mixture cool slightly, then whisk in the beaten egg yolks.

In a large bowl, beat the egg whites until they form stiff peaks. Add the cider mixture and fold gently together until evenly blended.

Pour into the prepared pie shell. Dust with the grated nutmeg.

Bake until the pastry is golden brown and the filling is well set, 30-35 minutes. Serve warm.

VERMONT BAKED MAPLE CUSTARD

—

USE 100% PURE VERMONT MAPLE SYRUP. COMMERCIAL VARIETIES ARE MADE MOSTLY OF CORN SYRUP AND WATER AND LACK THE INTENSE FLAVOR OF THE PURE SYRUP.

SERVES 6

3 eggs
½ cup maple syrup
2½ cups milk
⅛ teaspoon salt
⅛ teaspoon grated nutmeg

Preheat the oven to 350°F.

Combine all the ingredients in a large bowl and mix together well.

Set individual custard cups or ramekins in a roasting pan half filled with hot water. Pour the custard mixture into the cups. Bake until the custards are set, ¾-1 hour. Test by inserting the blade of a knife in the center: it should come out clean.

Serve warm or chilled.

CRANBERRY ICE

—

THIS ICE CAN BE SERVED AS AN ELEGANT PALATE FRESHENER BETWEEN COURSES AS WELL AS A GUILT-FREE DESSERT. GINGER SNAPS GO WELL WITH THE TART FLAVOR OF THE CRANBERRIES.

MAKES ABOUT 1½ QUARTS

2 quarts fresh or frozen
cranberries
2 cups water
1¾ cups sugar
¼ cups sugar
¼ teaspoon grated orange rind
2 tablespoons fresh orange juice

Check the manufacturer's instructions for your ice cream maker, if using one, to find out its capacity. If necessary, halve the recipe.

Pick over and wash the cranberries. Discard any that are blemished or soft.

Place the cranberries in a non-reactive pan with the water and bring to a boil. Reduce the heat and simmer until the berries soften, about 15 minutes.

Push the cranberry mixture through a fine-mesh nylon strainer set in a bowl. Return the purée to the pan, add the sugar, and stir to dissolve. Boil 5 minutes. Stir in the orange rind and juice. Remove from the heat and let the cranberry mixture cool. To freeze in an ice cream maker, pour the cranberry mixture into the machine and freeze following the manufacturer's instructions.

If you do not have an ice cream maker, pour the mixture into a metal or plastic freezer container and freeze until softly set, about 3 hours. Remove the mixture and chop roughly into 3-inch pieces. Place in a food processor and process until smooth. Return the mixture to the freezer container and freeze again until firm. Repeat this process 2 or 3 times, then leave to freeze until firm.

INDEX

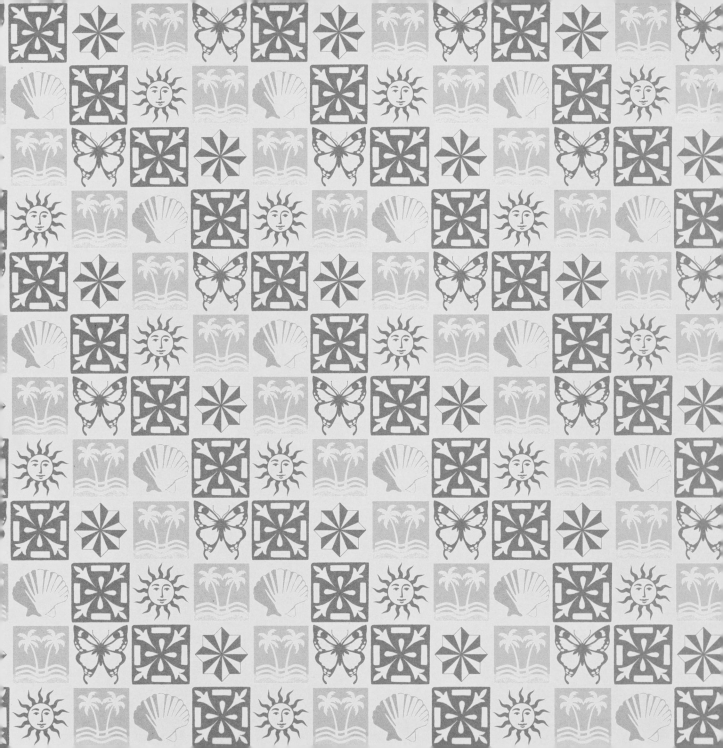